Sabrina Bri

Math Jones
Edited by Black Pe

First published in February 2018 by Black Pear Press
www.blackpear.net

ISBN 978-1-910322-61-1

Cover Design by Black Pear Press

Black Pear Press

Dedication

Many of these poems were written in and about Worcester, and in many ways owe their existence to the support and enthusiasm of the people of the Worcestershire literary world.

So my dedication is to the organisers, readers and audiences of such events as '42 Worcester', SpeakEasy, Parole Parlate, Word & Sound, Mouth & Music, The Phonic Kitchen, Earth Hour, Late to Lupercalia, Aurora Ostrealis, The Poetry Ballroom, The Literary Walks, and the Worcestershire Litfest & Fringe.

Testimonials

Math Jones writes like a troubadour, creating new myths that are bawdy, sweet and convincing. Wistfully rooted in contemporary life, his language ranges from secular medieval to the romantic poets, bringing us love, witchcraft, unfairness and revenge. A songbook for travelling players everywhere.
Kathy Gee

Sabrina Bridge contains wonder value. Math Jones weaves stories around his poems, explores the emotional landscape and plays with theatrical overtones. Writing in language that stands apart from everyday speech, emphasised by using particular metres and prosody, his classical poetry is a blending of emotions, intellect and sometimes love. This is a compelling read.
Nina Lewis—Worcestershire Poet Laureate 2017-2018

Math has a beautiful elegance with words, whether he is writing from a character's or his own perspective there is always something to learn about the human condition.
Jake Wild Hall—Boomerang Club, author of *Solomon's World*

A richly-textured evocation of a mythic, mystic world: Pagan folkloric and Pre-Raphaelite visions, pen-portraits of friends and poets, full of deep and dark enchantment.
Suz Winspear—Worcestershire Poet Laureate 2016-2017

Contents

If I Were Not

If I were not so wise a man
then I might be in love with you,
and all the pages of my book
would be just daisy petals on the wind.

Overheard From The Lover, Racing Past

I'm dizzy inside—with a glimmer round my eye—
and there is nothing about you unbeautiful.
The scent of the thought of you flips my heart over,
summons the holocaust, sends my heretic

racing to the chapel to pray, roaring to the gods
for more time in the dance, skimming down the hill
with one-mile bounds to catch at your absences,
places you were. Hugging myself, loving my self

because I love you, feeling clean in your smile
and deeply in love with your touch. I punch
the moment that takes you from me, jump-start
my life every time you arrive and freely, dive

headfirst into concrete or else into bliss,
should you offer a heartbeat, or brush off my kiss.

Sacred Calling

They walk, like pilgrims, on your skin, my fingers;
palms, cupped for alms, upon your hips, or pressed
in prayer, about your waist. Sweet incense lingers
on your breath: upon these lips, my faith professed.

A sacred heart within your bosom glows:
I place my hand, a scallop spread, divine
of touch; anoint the whiteness of your toes;
imbibe once more the miraculous wine.

Then eyes that saintly look, or angels' gaze,
with benediction, call as from my grave,
made whole, renewed, guided through end of days,
my soul in gold, baptismal waters bathe;

Your tongue on mine bestows the holy bread;
your body be the church for which I bled.

He Loved The Baker's Daughter

It not being sliced,
he would take out his knife
and, cupping the bloomer,

press in the blade,
drawing it down
one side like a zip,

exposing the soft and the white.
Then, laying flat
the thick, lush slab

he'd savour the surrender:
butter spread like lavished gold,
or kisses, drooling on the puffy bed.

Breaking the virgin crust,
he'd bite the spongy flesh,
as if it were a thigh.

In this way,
he would live
on her crumbs.

Map

I did not fall into love,
but walked, step by careful step,
down that precipitous path,
and if at times I stumbled
or sprinted, what of that?

I walked, and at each step
I mapped my course, set markers
on my road, to show perhaps
the journey back, but more
to know my journey in:

the dawn you brought; the music
sent, and doubtful glance; the laugh
behind each word and shielded;
fleet embrace; the stars caught
in your eye; my accent righted.

And if at times I faltered,
gave thought to retreat and run,
soaked in fear or disbelief,
your weightless touch or welcome
bore me further on,

past the catching briars, past
the dry and endless emptiness,
the desert beds of tearful streams,
the hollow skies, that would contain me
should I ever try to leave.

I did not fall. I walked,
and now I am arrived,
with map in hand, I wait,
unsure if you should join me
in this pitiless state.

Street Thief

He watched her leave her wealthy father's house;
walk arm in arm beside her aged nurse;
in admiration, gazed at this white mouse:
her pace, her form, her visage, and her purse;
and through the rutted streets, he dared pursue
the matron and her ward, upon their way:
the market square, the leafy avenue,
the churchyard, where her fallen mother lay.
And never, at the sights, did he espy
a look, or sideways glance, from out her eye.

He settled him beside a pauper's grave,
and wondered at her kneeling, fraught with grace,
the prayers that tripped, her mother's soul to save,
the thunder rolling 'cross her grieving face.
And thunder rolled across his breast, to see,
while lightning burnt the vision in his soul,
that such a one should weep so bitterly
for loss so young; that love should take such toll.
No more a thief, her weighty purse to dip,
unless to steal a smile from off her lip.

With flowers clenched in earnest fists, he came
to lay them in the urn, before the stone.
The wrinkled frown, it deepened on the dame;
The maiden, sign or notice gave she none.
He bent to take her hand, to offer aid
in lifting from the earth; she took it not,
but raised her head to his face as she prayed,
then turned away: so seen, so soon forgot.
The wizened dame alone did help her stand;
alone him left to nurse his stinging hand.

The gate he opened for them, chasing off
a crowd of beggars sat about the kerb,
then stopped the coach, and caught the shying horse,
forbidding hooves to bruise or she disturb.
Across the running stream, he laid his cloak,
his only shelter, to protect her shoe

and hem; the matron let the fabric soak,
and by another way, the lady drew,
who went as she was lead, without a word
or glance unto the boy who followed hard.

'Twas at the Market Cross, the cutpurse came,
with dagger bare, cold hunger on his lip,
slipped out the crowd and barged aside the dame,
to snatch the purse sharp from the young one's grip.
In darkness, stood alone, unseeing he
who robbed her of her guide, had cruelly ta'en,
from out her hand, her mother's rosary
and book of prayer, bequeathed when she was slain,
the poor girl reeled in terror and dismay
with naked, outstretched hands to find her way

and found rough fingers tipped with broken nails
calmly take hers, and in them softly press
the silken bag again; the nurse's wails
began to quiet; her own fear grew less,
as he whose heart was stole by she unseen,
whose care and deepest soul was snatched in kind,
saw now, with eyes devotional and keen,
this lovely street-thief girl had robbed him blind.
He helped the aged dame from where she'd tripped,
clutching tight at the wound the thief had ripped.

With whispered words, from breathlessness and pain,
he bled his heart's possession in her ear,
told the frantic woman his young sweet name,
how much he loved the girl: Tell her! Let her hear!
And falling, died; released the crabbed and wrinkled hand;
fell into the mud. The lady's shoes stained
forever, as she helped her guide to stand,
calmed her from grief, from questioning refrained,
even after weeks, why, security regained,
she, from her matron's eyes, felt water leak:
the nurse, for sure, was deaf and had no words to speak.

Dog, Roses

My love, she is so slender-oh,
as slender as the rose's wand;
and I would brave the keenest thorn
to hold her in my hand.

  My love, she is so dainty-oh,
  as dainty as the rose's hip;
  and though it scald my cupping hand,
  I'd bring her to my lip.

My love, she is beguiling-oh,
beguiling as the rose's scent;
and I would fill my lungs with her,
till breath is spent.

  My love, she keeps her secret-oh,
  as secret as the rose's bud;
  and I would blaze as bright as sun,
  to coax her from her hood.

My love has many faces-oh,
just as the rose has petals five;
and I would cut a swathe
to keep each one of them alive.

  My love is ever striving-oh,
  as striving as the rose's climb;
  and I would stand a hundred years
  to hold her flower high.

My love, she may be biting-oh,
as biting as the rose's worm;
but I would bear the canker's teeth,
to rescue her from harm.

  My love, her ways are jagged-o,
  as rose's leaf has jagged edge;

and I would drive my fleet aground,
to be her wrecker's catch.

My love, she has a hunger-oh,
as hungry as the rose's root;
and I would rot beneath the earth
to be her food.

The Rose Bird

for Deborah Rose

Upon a garden tower of stone and wood,
amidst a throng of autumn roses stood,
there lay a man of solid blood,
  full of sorrow, full of care.
New awakened in his bower,
from bitter dreams and visions dour,
he heard a note of gentle power—
birdsong of the waning hour,
  calling on the evening air—
delicate as dying flowers
  falling through the evening air.

Far softer than the velvet petal torn
and spread in tattered blanket o'er the lawn,
it caught him, like a sharp and hungry thorn,
  full of sorrow, full of care.
Climbing to the tower's height,
melancholy vying with delight,
it drew his gaze outward to the night
to seek whichever songbird might
  disturb the evening air:
sifting through a thickening light,
  he found no wren or linnet there,

but limp and sombre roses all around,
rooted in the heavy, guarded ground.
They nodded at the sound,
  full of sorrow, full of care,
and dripped their petals to the dew,
revealing not if any knew
the singer of that carol true:
the string of trilling music drew
  no answer from the air.
No keening bird of sorrow flew
  across the evening air…
A month and more in tower's loft,

he'd spent alone, repenting all he'd lost:
a love in ashes, turned to dust,
  gone to sorrow, gone to care,
and he lamenting on his woes,
but now into his window blows
a song to mourn the wilting rose.
Drawn by sweetened grief, he goes
  to plumb the tower stair,
descending as the darkness grows
  deeper in the evening air.

And hovered in the shadows at the door,
he silent stays a timid moment more,
to hear the haunting treble soar,
  in spite of sorrow, spite of care,
of how a love in heat of June
might turn upon a flower's bloom,
with raging thorns a guileless heart impugn,
and as so many petals strewn,
  be blown upon the summer air,
and spill upon the ground too soon,
  as if it never were.

As if such blossomed love had never been,
nor any kind of beauty seen,
but turned instead to scathing winter's dream.
So, full of sorrow, full of care,
he lashes at the bushes near,
the song of yearning in his ear.
Then with a step compelled by fear,
he trips, a foolish dumb career
  among the brambles there.
All rose and bud and foliage clear,
  the naked branches there.

Within his flailing hand he caught
a lonely branch of green and, fraught
with thorns, it punctured skin, and brought
  a cry of sorrow, keen despair.
With heart and head a hammer pounding,

welling from the stinging Mount
of Venus, blood in swelling fountain
fell in copious amount,
   a-dripping on the evening air—
bled through seven heartbeats' count,
   raining in the evening air.

Across the ground, the faded red
of roses, failing buds and petals shed,
as if from grievous woundings bled,
   so full of sorrow, full of care,
a kind of moulted plumage blown
and into nested piles grown,
it caught the gleaming raindrops thrown
like pips of pomegranates sewn
   across a field of evening air,
took the life-blood for its own,
   drinking in the evening air.

And on his back, the stars above,
his fingers clenched in bloody glove,
the final flutter of his love,
   last of sorrow, last of care,
let go the branch it clung upon;
taken by the setting sun,
witnessed by the silent moon,
dropped like roses' petals on
   the quiet of the darkened air,
floated in the sacred song
   that haunts the midnight air:

the song that glides on scarlet wings,
that from a rosebud-bosom sings,
the song that round the tower rings,
   not of sorrow, not of care—

but love and life to glorify!
As pinkly glows the dawning sky,
as bright as fire, in his eye
a bird of roses made, soaring high

across the morning air,
in velvet crimson, damask red, and crying
through the morning air

a song as secret as the furléd bud,
a song as hopeful as the opening bloom,
a song as splendid as the rampant flower,
a song as wise as the faded hue,
a song as sorrowed as the wilting head,
a song as jagged as a leafy edge,
a song with silence out of sound
of petals fallen to the ground.

The bird of fallen roses wheeled around
and vanished. Within the silence wound
another song, together bound
hope with sorrow, joy with care.
The saddened shadows fell away,
as from the trod and spotted clay,
arising with the morning ray
a rosebud new, winking at the day,
tried the brightening air,
and comfort in the briars lay,
full of beauty, full of care.

The Cause

I might have caused the sleeping earth to swell
and bloom, in velvet green, the hills to clothe;
to put out kissing buds and flowers fair—
but had not that power could make her love.

For me, the hare surrendered to the hound;
the fish for shame divorced the clinging sea;
but I, who offered riches to her choice,
lacked means to see that choice alight on me.

I bade the lyric find its melody,
the deaf and wordless poet learn to rhyme,
the painter's art to leap upon the page,
but could not take her heart, nor make it mine.

I caused the jealous sun to share its flame,
and coolness taught the rash and leerful moon;
I gave the first born his ancestral name;
wiped winter's nose; brought summer into June.

I walked with her beneath the bashful star
I'd minted new with heaven's keenest fire,
by living waters freshly squeezed from stone,
but had no means to make me her desire.

I could not make her love me, had no need:
the time of love she gave, she gave me free.

Puck In Love

after William Shakespeare's A Midsummer Night's Dream

…with Mustardseed. They kiss, of course—just tongues,
or lips, not both—keep something back. She sponges
dewdrops on his nose, and leads him, spirit,
up and down, a flaunty dance, a ringlet
through the brush and briar of her hair.
He hangs a pearl within her cowslip ear,
and, lurking in the bowl, cries raucous words
and jellywinks, adorning her with curds.

Morning finds them crept into acorn cups,
on the ground, sleeping sound and holding hips.
They take the night as blanket, play "Athenians
i'the Wood" and "Scratchy-Scratchy" o'the green.
O'er they fall, till once again, Aurura comes.
Cobweb blows a raspberry, and shows her bum.

Perhaps it was the watching of her scratch
the ass, the ear, the Queene of Faerie's catch,
that did bestir a monster to be moved
or else beware. Or was it Idle-Love,
still smeared on mitts unwashed and wiping tears
of laughter from his cheeks did her endear
and stain the knavish lob with purple wound?
But tired heart or fired tongue, he swoon'd.

Alas, no almanac is found can tell
us aught of the mechanics of it all,
(though certain 'tis a moon did shine that night:
a dream without a bottom holds the sprite!)
Th'Athenians did it! With rough-cast and mirth!
And now is placed a girdle round the earth.

The Magic Pig

to the tune of The Barley and the Rye

Mistress Margery was a lonely wife,
Though she kept her lodgings full:
Sweet bacon back, sure, thank you, ma'am,
For the feeding of us all.
The inker-man, and the candle-man,
The cog-man and the fool:
Sweet bacon back, sure, thank you, ma'am,
For the feeding of us all.

Every Saturday, with her porker,
She would walk out on the moor,
And return with a bag of bacon back,
For to feed her lodgers four.
And her husband dear, the gallows-man,
Gazed in silence from the wall;
Sweet bacon back. Sure, thank you, ma'am,
For the feeding of us all.

'Twas the cinder-man, who spied on her,
Walking Saturday, on the moor.
Said, I've seen you with your porker,
Lying naked on the floor.
Would you have me write to your gallows-man,
Would you have me stories tell?
Sweet bacon back, I'll be thanking thee
For the feeding me as well…

Oh, this bacon back, it is salty.
This bacon back, it is dry.
Will you tell us all, gentle mistress,
Why the weeping of your eye?
The inker-man and the candle-man,
The cog-man and the fool;
Sweet bacon back, please tell us, ma'am,
The meaning of it all.
So, on Saturday, with her porker,

She walked sadly on the moor,
And the cinder-man, keen to follow her,
Was surprised by lodgers four,
And the townspeople saw him running,
With a face of ash and ill.
Sweet bacon back? No, thank you, ma'am,
I have surely had my fill.

Mistress Margery was a thankful wife,
When she walked next on the moor,
And her porker ran beside her,
Smiling up at her from the floor,
And she thanked her kindly husband,
For the piglet prodigal.
Sweet bacon back, we'll be thanking thee,
For the feeding of us all.

Suzerain

for Suz Winspear

She has grown feather-boned. From such as she
they harvest corset-stays, swan's-neck slender,
whale-bone strong, with the lost simplicity of lace.

As rich as lace in her history, intricacy,
possessing now the delicacy of cloud
in a blue sky, and sunshine fragility

upon a whited shoulder, a fine weave of skin,
lightly dusted with lines. What hangs between
the spider-arms of the parasol should not be taken in.

Strong enough still to thrust stitches through leather,
with crow's razor-bill and -claw; to strangle with a corset-cord.
Preening raven feather and brocade,

her eyes are a veil to hide her face.
Her teeth have a tender bite, delicate in taste.

The Heathen Girl

She did not seem a wild girl;
a wild girl she did not seem,
though she was armed with knives, and eyes
that rose from out my deepest dream.

She carried too a sark of shame;
a sark of shame she had beneath
the modest dress and cloak demure
she wore to walk upon the heath.

A father's strict and stern belief,
she sought escape from on the heath.

At her request, I followed on;
I followed her some steps behind:
her basket held upon my arm,
desire held within my mind—

desire full, that I might with
my arms her slender form ensheathe;
might lay her down and make her mine
for just two hours on the heath.

or like a Jack-in-Green bequeath
some seed of love upon the heath.

Upon a mossy bank we stayed;
we stayed upon a bank of moss,
and there within the sun's kind rays
she sang me of her love and loss.

Her love and loss, and keen despair
she showed; I sheltered in her grief,
and waited for the storm to pass,
to offer comfort on the heath;

to lay her on the ground beneath,

and show her comfort on the heath.

I rested then upon her breast;
upon her breast, I soundly slept,
her shaken legs around me wrapped,
and on my cheek the tears she wept.

Then down my cheek the salt tears ran,
slipped lightly over lips and teeth,
played on my tongue a salty tang,
for to revive me on the heath,

or morelike, as a murdrin' thief,
to poison me upon the heath.

She opened up her basket then;
her basket then she opened wide
and, with the blade which lay within,
she cut my heart from out my side.

She cut my heart and laid it bare,
whilst with my curls she made a wreath,
and set them in the basket there,
to carry me across the heath:

a bed of young hearts underneath
my own, her cargo on the heath.

Revenant

The air here is too still to hold
anything but the dead.
I am the only agitation.
And the room is too cold
to house anything fed.
This I know without hesitation.
Everything here was foretold
in the passages read;
this, mere confirmation.

The sense of absence is real
among these greying weights.
In stillness I remain a disturbance.
Whatever life they were willing to feel,
whatever selfless fates
they kept, they've lost them to silence.
While I wait to un-congeal
my blood, my body dis-coagulates,
prepares to end this awful abstinence.

Sight is unnecessary.
Sound also. Only scent adheres.
And taste, upon the breath.
Something beyond stands as promissory.
Felt in jellied veins, it nears
this pitied chamber of death:
a calm missionary,
ready to spill into our ears
prayers to the lamb of Nazareth.

Transition is near complete,
the ritual close to done.
No action required,
other than to drink, to taste meat:
to let the blood run
through a heart long expired,
and this sodden corpse reheat.

Another disentombed son.
Another first breath respired.

This moment of lying still,
aware, not yet alive,
will be my last repose,
knowing that from this, I must kill,
devour, if I would thrive.
And never more dispose
myself to sainted sleep, until
the final days arrive,
and the blessed dead have all arose.

The Wail Of The Banshee (The Bean Sidhe)

There is a cold, hard voice
blowing at the doors;
this is why
I burn my heart so fierce.

A cold, hard cry
sweeping round the eaves;
for this
I keep my head so high.

A bone-dry scratch
against the window pane;
and so
I set my passion to the match.

A cold and empty roar
cries harsh against the wall,
and this is why
I slip the latch,

my dress,
and dance,
dance
naked on the moor.

Macbeth (Hecate's Summons)

after William Shakespeare's Macbeth

Was not the raven hoarse that croaked? Did not
three midnight hags, their choppy fingers take
from skinny lips to speak? Was all so wrought
and freely too, this! for a kingdom's sake?

What might be done? What more, when time and place
shall make themselves? The dagger warns, "Proceed
no further. Hold, enough!" The petty pace
cries not: "Thus thou must do, this nameless deed!"

Has not the old man so much blood in him,
and will not blood have blood? A wayward son,
fall'n down upon a step, his stars so dimmed,
"Prince Cumberland", enkindled to a crown...

Or who can say what murd'ring sleep will bring?
Wait! but one night! and night may make you king.

Bean Nighe

after William Shakespeare's Macbeth

What woman that, knelt beside the flood, hands
plunged deep into red water? What cloth
does she beat upon the stones? What cold strands,
bloody strings of clotted threads, from old swaddling?

Is't the queen then so piteously bent,
unsucked, heavy dug? She would have been mother
to so many—*No, lord, the queen is dead*—
MacDuff, then! Has she the look of his beloved,

scrubbing up her children from the floor? She
never came to court. I would not know her,
I would not—*Please, my lord, who do you see?* —
A woman ne'er known stands now to show her

torn tatters of a womb, her belly ripped,
memory, of a babe she never knew, gripped.

Bradán

Know, I have only so many years left to me,
and never another today,
while you still have forever,
like the salmon in the river—
always, there's a salmon in the water;
you would think it were immortal,
though some fisherman will catch this one hereafter.

From his place within the sheltered pool,
seeing glints of you and shadows
on the pebbling below, he might deem
you 'eternal man'—always, a man on the shore:

each staring eye upon the endless stream,
each perhaps forgetting the source and the sea.

Late To Lupercalia

You see, I have danced
with the blood-flecked women
and they did not te
ar me. Perhaps they were tired,
from frenzy. One kissed me
and iron of him was upon her,
dribbled down her chin.

I was late too for Lupercalia,
though a wolf-boy lea
pt, my heart in his mouth,
and we danced amongst the skins
scattered on the ground.
Did he scamper, or I,
howl-like bowling through the town?

No poet. No lover.
All of us late to cre
ation stories. Still,
it keeps me company:
the blood on a Maenad's
throat, on a wolf's tongue,
salting everything I eat.

Sorge (Sor-ye)

It is never behind you;
it is always within you,
like the rings in a tree,
or a knot in the wood,
disguised by the bark,
but still showing through—
a branch that never grew.

love stubborn

it's not the wound still raw that draws the rage
but more the thought of nature's healing scab
rough and ugly cover, an angel's cage
to keep the sore inside, a livid crab
pinching, clinging on, the hurt to assuage
flaking then from skin made whole and drab

the fire aches to burn, the flame to soar
the purple bruise to bloom upon the snow
the blood to splay across the stricken floor
the neck's blue vein to open to the blow
and ever all and each desire more
than see this love and ardour turn and go

Love Note

We do not not always notice
what gifts lay may before us:
the words of love been spoken
by the friend I stood at our side.
And meaning care made so plain
in the words of for love we've woken
are so often felt you unnoticed
in the storm of shouted hurts and tears cried.

Unstained

Though I have lived a life of shame
and death, within the brambled wood,
still, I hold this flower for you,
unstained with blood.

Silver-white it glistens still,
around a heart of coppered gold,
which never darkness' hand could steal,
nor shadow hold.

I have it for you, here, among
the grit and thorn, and while the bed
of rivers slowly chokes with slaughter,
dammed by the dead,

to tally all the wounds, the shreds
of every cull, I slice still more
into the root, and feed the tender curl
the tears I draw.

Beneath this frowning canopy,
when all the dolour of the world
has spat, I bit them back, and kept
your secret furled.

I keep it still, the only bloom
that I could ever grasp, and this
a kindness never shown unto
another's kiss.

These Are My Secrets

I.

I take no step through these caverns.
  I do not breathe,
  and my heart is muffled too.
I float, in a way that is not there,
  from stillness to stillness,
  and I carry no light.
I see because it is mine to see,
  each thing as a variant of darkness,
  each thing as a variance of density,
  some more still than other still,
  but each the centre of all that may be.
There is no sound, but this mute song,
  the noise of being there.
  I hold my gravity like breath,
  so as not to pull the silence from the air.
  If air there is…Whatever fills the void
  that is no void, it might be bliss,
  but I will not let it move my lung.
These are my secrets.
These are things I cannot bring into the day,
  and struggle with at night
  and at the door to death.
  They may even be keeping me alive.

II.

Could I walk with you here?
  In blindfold?
Cover your ear?
  Stop your nose?
  Carry you?
  Dribble air into your mouth
  from mine?
And say never a sound?
Even then I fear you'll feel the tender

in a difference of the heat
or cold,
should I bring you too near.
These are my secrets.
I have no way
to make them clear to me,
much less to you.
But I could not bear to love you so,
and not let you know
they are there.

First published in *Word Up Anthology* vol. 1, 2016

Things My Lover Says

My lover says I'm a dark forest,
and sometimes she must keep within the garth,
for the howls of wolves and bear's growling,
and the shadow's fall across the path.

But other seasons bring a better comfort,
with the birds' tune sweetly in the air,
over mossy beds, a fresh and verdant canopy,
beams with blossom for her hair.

And I would be the forest to surround her
and hold her in the branches of my care.

My lover says I'm a brooding mere,
and sometimes she must stay upon the shore,
when the cold face, iron-still and mirrored,
carries silent clouds scudding, nothing more.

But other weathers bring a kind reflection,
of glistened diamonds sparking to a flame;
gentle splashes captured with a dash of white,
showing clear to the heart, and tame.

And I would be the water to refresh her,
to bathe her, and give her back her name.

My lover says I'm a distant mountain,
and sometimes she must linger in the dale,
for the roll of the wind and the savage troll,
the cliffs too dire for the fleet goat to scale.

But other days allow a new perspective,
as the rain washes silver down the fall,
and a softer shoulder of earth will lift the view
on a world, leave one ruler of it all.

And I would be the foothold that might raise her,

and the herd to answer to her call.

My lover, she's a whispering ocean,
and sometimes I must rest upon the strand,
learning from the secrets she will tell me,
the letters she has washed upon the sand.

Though other moons may stir her into tempest,
may draw her, ebbing, from the beach,
with the pearl and the coral and the whale's cry
behind a sharp wave, caught and out of reach,

still, I will stand alone upon the harbour
as I must, to hear the song she will teach.

The Gift

She sent a penny to her love,
but wrapped in gold and silver lace,
enclosed within an ermine glove,
and locked inside a walnut case

entrusted to a herald bright,
new-mounted on a gleaming mare,
all guarded by a prince's might
upon the kingly highway fair,

and through a rich and rolling land
she sent her promise to his hand.

He left the highway where it lead,
the warlike royal guard dispersed,
the snorting steed unbridléd,
released the herald unrehearsed,

embarked the vessel walnut wood
and let the wild ermine roam,
gave out the gold for pauper food
and silver-laced the beggar's tomb;

he kissed the copper-tarnished face,
and called her to a last embrace.

The Flood

I gripped upon the ragged bank,
the brimming water in my eye,
that carried all most sacrosanct,
the flooded river by

And how the captain's mounted troop
came rearing to retrieve the shore,
unhorsed they each, by stallions' stoop,
that never rode more

And all the bishop's pated kin,
upon the cross's height engripped,
baptismal waters washed again
and from them stripped

I never saw the moneyer's wifc,
for sure she could not swim, nor float,
though he was paying for his life,
the gold within his boat

The king stayed on his castle's top,
holding to the realm that his remained,
crying to the tide: Hear me! Stop!
The waters he disdained

But she, I saw, from her tower
leaping, with a free and falling cry
her dresses spread, an open flower,
to greet a lover's eye

Welcome in the river's hard embrace
I saw her swirling in his arms
carried like a swan, from drowning safe
and all other harms

At last, the river's grip was more
than mine, and into waves I sank,
carried, by his daughter, from the shore,
most sacrosanct.

Caught In A Storm

Once more I turn to the storm for guidance.
Where else would I find such all-things-are-true?
Where else is such forbearance:

one for celebration, one for rue,
one for dancing no-legged in the rain,
one for tearing thunder from a heavy blue?

Contradicting winds vie across the main,
lightning thinks itself and blinks away,
waters well and mither from the drain,

red and black pour bruises on the grey,
churning nervous clouds clap to the drum,
the night is giving birth, and the green day

surrenders gladly to the horsemen come
to tear the field, a thousand lances
landing with a cannonade's thrum...

The huddled foxes sharing warning glances
at the roots around them roaring to the sky,
Take us, now! The dolmen's trances,

jolted all anew, sensing emptiness, decry
the theft of grave and dancing bone,
the dead and empty tomb would fly

the heady stone
into a bedded sea.
And so never be alone.

Beneath the hills, the giant whimpers, leave us be.
The dragon child starts to teethe.
The gods all gather, come in silence to the tree.

Quiet threads its way across the weave,
the needle's eye of calm
will have its time amongst the seethe,

bringing to the boil a breathing balm,
balanced on the high point and the low,
and still the battened cry, Alarm , Alarm!

I, suspended on the edge of shall I stay, should I go,
throw myself upon her roiling majesty,
swept across the cauldron sky, to know

the size and quiet thunder we may be,
the heavy rain and weightless flash of thought,
the callous love and tender fury,

the vagaries of all our many weathers brought
to bear in one still moment of life,
and, in one calm moment of decision, caught.

January

It being resurrection month,
the sleep before life, many may deny it,
but January is undoubtable bone.

It is a heavy eyelid time: *let me sleep*
just an hour, let me dream of warmer weather,
let me snooze, let her kiss me just once more.

Sleep, by all means. The milkman of the year
will not have harnessed up his horse.
The world around you dozes under snow;

the men will not be fishing yet,
but under ice, the river rolls.

Black Pheasant Hen

I felt the thud.
which maybe only the living feel,
and thought not that I'm about to die,
but that I'm about to kill,
and though I slowed for the bird,
and she would have made it past,
she stopped
and looked at me, still too fast
to stop myself,
and it became braking so as to kill her safely,
in control of my vehicle,
and she had given herself up to be killed
for the Earth, my lover,
as I'd given up myself in the field,
and then the rain covered over us both.
But I felt the bump,
as I hit a black split into the road,
and continued
on my way.

Hawk

I wanted you to see me,
watched you from a distance
and stood in plain sight
—an attempt at reassurance,
but to you perhaps,
dear rabbit, as welcome
as the kestrel's hovering flight.

I wanted you to see me,
an invitation, allowing you the means
to approach when you chose—
knowing our meeting was inevitable—
but perhaps for you
it was simply a glare of headlights
in which you froze

So I took a moment to near you,
swooping into contact,
focused hawk-like upon your shoulder
turning
coldly
away from me
slamming me flat
into the hood of the oncoming truck.

I cannot let you see me now,
thrown bloody on the roadside,
feathers bent and broken, one wing torn
from me. The moment was mischosen.

First published in *Decanto Magazine*, December 2012

Love Lines

Love lines incised in the side of my hand:
the palm-reader's art reveals one to be
you. If it be so, then you have been here,
a crease in my skin, since first it clothed me.

If it be so, and you were foretold by
a fold, layers deep, then still you remain
(more real than time, as I grow around you),
carved in my grip, since before I knew when;

since before my heart first learned how to love
and then forget. Though I could not grasp you,
walking together, my line in your hand
held your line in mine, and no scratch or tear

(for I can't dig you out) will ever be so fixed
as that line in my palm, the deepest, longest.

First published in *Ripples Anthology*, 2012

A Gathering Of Poets At The Old Rectifying House

You would think it a place
where things are put right,
where mistakes are redressed
and looseness made tight,
where ancient misdoings
were brought to the light.

Crouched by the river,
on the shoulder
of the bridge, this brick and timber
palace of The Old
Rectifying House
sits like a scolder!

But here, the judgements made
put no one in a pillory,
were on refinement, grades
of alcoholic purity,
the wash of fermentation
for the Williams Distillery.

Spirits of over 90% proof!
Stilled and redistilled,
might have took the roof
of any fool willed
enough to drink it. 'Struth!
How many coffins filled?

Still! The spirits here
were recondensed 90% pure.
Might not those other spirits,
the quiet ones, hid behind the door,
or in the beams, give us writers welcome,
our writings to endure?

The Butts

What an archer she was.
  Smack!
She hit, and the tip was hot.
  Smack! She hit again,
in the exact same spot.
  Smack! With a third,
she split the shaft.
  Smack!
Again, and this time, laughed.
  Smack!
This arrow trick's getting old.
  Smack! Smack! Smack!
Feet are getting cold…
  Smack!
Festooned,
like a hedgehog at a wedding feast,
  Snack, snack, smack!
A porcupine on honeymoon!
  Smack. The last dart, surely,
falling from above—
  Smack—
The last of a million ways
she had me fall in love.

Faithful

In a little Powick cottage
on the road to Upton Town,
my love beside her bonny boy
does lay her body down,
while I above old Bedwardine
do slumber with my own.

Upon a morning, first of May,
her road did cross with mine:
across the ancient battlefield
the meeting of our eyen,
her bonny lad high on the cart,
and she did walk behind.

And at the bridge we passed,
I standing back to clear her way;
a simple smile on her cheek,
that newly broke the day.
Her breath did catch, and mine was caught,
upon that morn in May.

And each at each did gaze behind
across the winding river Teme,
and walked with backward step,
the day adrift upon the stream,
a thread to hold our fingers well
as any glover's seam.

That time and on, her secret's kept,
and mine is kept as well,
though loud my heart within my breast
as this cathedral bell,
and none shall know the wishes
I must to the river tell.

My hand within the water
leaves no writing to be read.

My voice upon the beacon—
none to witness what I've said.
The vows of Nunnery reveal
no trace of where I tread,

while in a Powick cottage
on the road to Upton Town,
my love beside her bonny boy
must lay her body down,
while I above old Bedwardine
do slumber with my own.

The Battlefield

Do you not fear, father, that the soldiers
will rise again from the field in anger?
When flood has come and gone its way,
I sometimes see the whites of their remains
digging through the clay, and when the wind
assails the trees, or running under storm,
I often hear their yells or cannonade
across the Vale. I fear their harm.

Hush, girl. Tomorrow morn, you'll follow me
behind the horse, and as the harrow breaks the dirt,
it crumbles too the bones by each furrow thrown,
ploughs them back into the earth. Who would want
but to go back into the ground he died upon,
with comrades all around and foemen too—
a commonwealth amongst the tilth. Leave the clutching
of your gown; your mother's close. Sleep a child's dream.

I've heard them, father, buffet at the doors
and at the gentle windowpane, dance the smoke
back down the chimney, wanting in, wanting out again.
Felt it in my frock clamped across my thigh,
and in the blood I shed. Felt against my chest.
My mother lies amongst them: I see the earth disturbed
around her grave, and there is marching in my ear
as I lay myself to rest. Father, I fear.

You've never strode, Miss, upon a battle's
scarred and sorry earth, seen the soldiers knotted
on the ground, arm in arm, in bloody grip,
with innards ripped and lying in a tangle all around,
the captain trapped beneath his horse, and by his own command
garotted. None is so binded, one to other,
as soldiers in the fray, in slaughter as in laughter.
To rise against those who know it not, is not the soldier's way…

Misting The Malverns

for Polly Stretton

This mist is a visible silence,
swallowing dogs and letting
voices run a mile. While steep
is just as steep and breath
as short as sight: the views
have been rubbed out! What an eraser!

Everywhere is an edge of the world!
Single trees lurk, like Orsenian spies
beneath grey gaberdines,
smoking, nicotine-free;
the rocks and out-crops
comb over their woven rugs;

and the peaks, in brilliant green,
(glad to be the only thing to be seen)
are preening.
  The sculptor in bronze
has been free with the bracken:
they keel over and sing, "Look at us!
We're dying! Isn't it exciting!"

The tuffets are having a party,
(or forming a party—militant
molehills draped in silver—
"Why must we stay here all year,
whilst shrubbery takes a holiday..?")

Across the dyke, splitting the difference,
to one side, Uncestershire,
to the other, Unfordshire:
if you walked down one slope,
you'd only walk under and come up the other...

Immense and round, brighter than white,
the sun has crept close, a virginal girl
gazing through muslin (or else, nosey neighbour,
twitching the curtain). She thinks she's unseen,
self-conscious of her size.

Paths criss-cross, ropes made in Lilliput,
walked by a laureate, weighted by benches:
unanchored, the hills would float free.

Worcestershire Beacon

In search of New Year, we stumbled upon
Beacon Lane, in the dark. A stream of people,
wrapped and booted, led the way; butterfly
lamps and fairy lights in a cavernous sky.

Rising over a flattened earth (every hill
in the world was here), climbing blacker ground,
steeped in shadow, a clipped-penny half-moon
and stars were all out-stared by city glare.

We sat upon an unseen bank, the wind
above and unseen people all about
(counting down the time and pressing drinks
into my hand), watched fireworks like raindrops.

We missed the path descending, saw the streams
to right and left, took baby steps, arm in arm.

Malvern Hills

Can she feel, this fierce dragon of earth,
(roaring up from the river plain, making
a skyline, throwing our shadows over
the valley floor), the tread of our footsteps?
I think mine travel too lightly, holding your hand.
Does she notice the weight of my clinging,
upon her back, stroking the down of her ear,
whiles you, lain on mine, rest like sunlight,
a weight of warmth only, and share your breath.
As the wind whips your hair into thorns and willows,
rootless here, does she feel (this one, outlasting
so many) the screaming desire for you
to stay? To stay…The beacon is burning.

Worcester In Flood

The bridge is in the water thigh deep—
couldn't roll his trouser high enough
to keep 'em dry: a wading fisherman,
trawling up a timber isle for ducks to sleep.

The swans have become royalty, the queens
and kings, and princelings, bossy on the Quay:
visiting the homes of more humble birds,
among the sunken branches of flood plane trees.

It might be old-time market day:
just so many brown backs pushing down the cattle track—
a canal of cows, a herd of water—
past the Cattle Market and on their way.

Roads have been erased. Venice-like,
everything has dropped beneath her smooth face,
the Welsh water, coached in from the mountains
for a Christmas Fayre. She has spread herself wide.

Fish invade the Pitchcroft, racing now
with soft going round the parked and sunken cars;
and the fence juts white like a dragon's ribs,
water-wyrm's skeleton in soggy ground.

The river eyes the beacon, dreams of Glastonbury Tor,
not so far, not so high, could she gather
for the future, bring her boar and her cattle,
all her swans and her salmon, make those hills no more

than an island..?

Sabrina

I bring you news of the mother's river's daughter, flaring with the burnish of the water's ruddy hair, tresses in the spirals, herding whorls, flurried strands, laughter on the beaches, reaches with a heavy wrinkled grip…

Born beneath rock, drawn from caves, this king's daughter
learns to walk   in darkness, wrinkly knees and serried palms
upon the splashy floor, splattered yaps and milk cries.

Little lips tasting pools dribbled small from stalactites,
crinkled fingers for a better grip, laughter ripples
over lakes, wet black skipping under dank black.

Only smoky love to show her mother's eyes, rubies flaring
in the dark, her daughter's grin the brightest thing there is,
running gladly into deepness, dark, the known unseen:

every inch of darkness ever known and all the new gradations
of the deep; the cracks within the smoothness of the rock,
not thin enough to stop her fingers' laughing prying.

When news came of her father's wife's passing, doors were opened high above. She wondered at the steps prepared by man, at the sponginess of wood, of metal blistered by her water's touch.

Burst from the well, she breaks into epiphany of air,
bubbles out of dankness, darkness banished by the first kiss of sun,
a second kiss of warmth calling back the heavy wet,

screaming at the sun's rush in overjoy, sharp delight
at the shaping rays of light falling lightly onto lines
and beds and colours, light abounding in her cry, and into day.

Light, dancing like a falling thing, she overflows across the floor,
running over prickly mats of straw, wearing toes and heels raw
over dry stone and wooden board, roaring over grass,

blades between her toes, rolling with the daisies and the buttercups—
sinking is a new thing, sinking into soil, little white rooty fingers catching
earth beneath the nails and filling all the runnels of her palm's lines with
dirt.

When news came of her father's wife's brother's anger, an army raised, another come in league, the king moving swift to meet them each before they join, she wondered at the noise, of the rolling siege machines, sparks from off the cavalry hooves.

Here's the rain dripping from the cavern of the sky.
Here's her looking for the stalactite, and catching raindrops
on her clothes, her tongue, her wide-flung eye.

Fingers wrinkled, dancing as the earth swells, softens, takes
the wheels of the urgent army, slows the feet
of the crew, as she throws her arms astride.

Her bright, white body sticking to the flimsy, thirsty cloth,
shining through the cloud, cannot steal the fear,
the sod, from the heavy soldiers, sinking in their gear.

A leaky cup, her father's army, soon dashed empty
by the flood of foes; her father's head soon skimming over sward.
She marvels at the red, splashed, of battle, all the golden slaughter.

No news was brought of what her father's wife's brother, her father's killer, had in mind for the harlot's daughter. She watched the red intoxicate the earth, fly in her father's hair, settle like a crimson robe around the falling sun.

Cold, windless falling under silver moon skies, her mother
stands, a stone wall, a single window showing out the fire,
carried swift away by the roaring river (another new thing), and sunken
down, drowned.

Her father's lover's daughter carried now by muscled arms
and warm, ringed with gold, rippling all with iron blood
and fired air, and flecked with brooding, downy hair;

heat and sweat beneath her wrinkled grip, carries her
to the nameless river's edge. With eyes low as a cavern pool,
he casts her high, every colour in the sky, into the rush.

The touch of water brings her home and into darkness,
deeper, dazzling, never known, this surge of water flowing.
Fingers wrinkle, get a grip on every drop wheeling in the feeling dance…

Blodeuwedd—Tales from The Mabinogion

Made of flowers? Did you make me, wise Math
ap Mathonwy, wizard prince of Gwynedd?
To void a shamed mother's wrath? Three times tricked,
Arianrhod; did you see her, and laugh?

Once to gain a name: was it good, unknown
to bring the skilled shoemaker? His deft-stone-
killing from a fair-hand thrown? Gwydion giggling
at his cleverness; his sister left alone?

Twice to gain a sword, to bring a false tale
of siege, with a false bard, her son, to regale;
his very song betrayal? She buckled
on the blade herself! Oh, no, you could not fail!

A tynged sharp bequeathed to save her life,
three times spoke, the angry words: neither knife,
nor shield, nor name he'd have—unless bestowed
his mother by—nor any human wife!

So for your niece's son, your sister's son's
sister's son, you gathered oak, chestnut, broom
for maiden's hair, hawthorn too: nine wild flowers…
And named me Blodeuwedd, the earth in bloom;

given in gift to Lleu Llaw Gyffes then,
whom death would never visit, only when…
And his mother's mind scorned again! Did you think
I would not dare take my own choice of men?

Now I will screech and howl in the dark wood,

my wide flower-face bright under night's hood,
take the mouse and vole for food, scare the other
birds with the scathing glower of my mood.

Though you may deem thyself a woman's maker,
formed of flowers, letting not a harsh wind shake
her, for her beauty's sake—be wise, Math
ap Mathonwy! Her choice is never yours to take!

Rhiannon—Tales from The Mabinogion

Riding at unhurried pace a white horse,
She, clad in gold; me, a race
behind, caught in a blind chase.

Her, with gleam on cloth and hair, undisturbed
by wind or travel; I despair,
bite hard upon a blighted air.

She, seated tall and sedate, untroubled
by the miles; I, close to dead,
in haste, curse the waste ahead.

She at ease, through summer grove and heather-
banked moors, lightly stepped; I move
screaming limbs, and dreaming love.

Steady on the mountainside, and quiet
as the valley, Her sigh; ride
I an avalanche, staunch pride.

And gentle as the last wave over sand,
She, light as spray; my craving
Her or else my early grave—

Horse & rider lose their way—She alone
disappearing like the day—
Lady, cried at last, please stay!

On the far road She, disappeared in mist,
turns into a voice severe,
fiercely present—She is here!

Goewin—Tales from The Mabinogion

My name is Math. I must to keep my life
rest my feet in a girl's lap,
both willing and no one's wife,

unless there be inclemency of war.
With you, Goewin, I remain,
gently held, the land secure.

But sister's son, Gilfaethwy, you have caused
the fighting calls me away;
with your brother, Gwydion, forced

the doors and took the maid against her say—
all heard her shouts of protest!
Goewin, I ask, with me stay,

to take the might of Gwynedd for your own,
queen of my land, queen of Math,
that right for you may be done.

Too-clever Gwydion, what is to do
to mete out vengeance over
each, your false brother and you,

you pair, but pare you down, and pair you up
as hart and buck, boar and sow,
each to bear the other's pup.

You're turned to hind with hide of fired gold,
your brother to stag, chasing
over hill till son is foaled.

Your brother is turned to sow in woods wild,
rooting now with you as boar
to litter a piglet child.

Turn you next to bitch, your high silver yelp
calls your brother wolf: howl through
mountaintops till son is whelped.

You came to me holding your own want higher!
If you must burn, I'll make you
yearn for what you least desire.

Forest Poet

for Jenny Hope

He never found her person in the woods.
But saw the signals of her passing by:
the sister's gaze she'd settled on the trees;
her tread within the brook; the pebble's sigh;

her kiss upon the yew; the owl's distress;
the song she'd given the halt crow to sing;
the grove found only where she'd slipped her dress
in tryst with her lover, the forest wind.

Only this he'd found: a shelter of stick,
ash, oak and elm upon the leafy floor,
a woven house, of branch embound with twig,
of birch-bark, holly-green and sycamore:

knotted words, with willow stitched, interspersed
with elder rhymes, to make her heart-wood verse.

First published in *Be Magazine*, 2012

Quartet

I.

In silence, I came to the whispering cave,
found echoes hung within the scathing void,
a seething emptiness, with voices brave
and rare, clamouring for a turn of tide.

It is the meeting place, he cried, *of dreams*
from the deep and the rocks that will wreck them,
the place where words are bound, are put to screams
in dancing bows, the better to forsake them!

Words writ in sand, he said, *will fade and pass,*
(spilling gasoline across the cavern floor);
I'll set a blaze to melt the sand to glass,
and stop the tide-spun poet writing more.

I saw the shattered dreamer, with his fear,
applauded, by those gathered round to hear.

II.

I came, with reverent step, to the chaste well,
churning vertigo sat upon its lip:
light defeated, compelling secrets tell
their stories, rising from the river's grip.

The water's foul, she promised, *tip it out*
your cup; too many bodies tumbled in
and left their smear; too many, caught in drought
or sorry flood, have let the waters thin.

Waters drawn unwilling from the deep, must
She said, *have in them wicked iron, red*
with warning skies; the chalice words will rust
themselves away, their golden liquid bled.

The water bearer sank beside her wilted urn,
too weary now, to from her watchers turn.

III.

I came in peace to the blistering sky,
placed my ear, soft, to the lips of the wind,
whose easing chatter kissed, bit, and full shy,
flew once more, where, off-hours, silence dinned!

Do not believe, the raven cawed, *the truth*
of noise. Veracity is rare. Be sure
that bones will make a song when shaken; tooth
will draw a scream from out the sceptic maw!

I make a meal of that most carrion sound:
the poet's dead and empty phrases line
my peckish gut, easy pickings, not found
where preyers bow to tear the sound divine.

The priestly blackbird swooped to have my eye;
I left him choking, on a vision dry.

IV.

At last, I found my way to the tower's height,
a vault on vaults, and steeped within the view
were songs of sacred chemistry, alight
with falling comets, scarring on the blue.

The Word is lost, I heard the heavens mourn,
and it was good, though now it falls away,
among so many tongues; the shepherd shorn
of psalms to plead my case on Judgement Day.

What use is but one word, they cried, *when time*
is not enough to have it said. Reduce
the stark vocabulary more and rhyme
shall go extinct, nor angels' wings produce.

The secretariat had copies read
of every word, wrote prophet on its head.

V.

At poem's end, the keeners stood about
and cast their ash upon the closing line,
lowered to the pit the last crazy shout
of angry flesh, thought on heat, tasted wine.

Always hid beneath, the buried sang, *falling*
through the holes, and rising with the moon's lack,
to gambol under eaves and still our calling,
within the darkest spaces at your back.

I shift the earth to fill my rotted frame,
make puddles full of night and liquid shade;
the virgin stone, that never bore my name,
exhales and trembles, seeing justice paid.

Nor cave, nor well, nor sky, nor tower's clip,
will tell or bid the next word from my lip.

The Beggared Troubadour

A man may have too many loves and yet
one more might bring him home, might let him know:
that, in the ragged days, he did not miss
the door, the silhouette wrapped in fire's glow,

on roads so far behind he'd never reach
so much as faintest memory of where
that crossing stood, nor have the feeling hands
to touch her softest skin, or thrilling hair.

Upon another threshold, knuckles boned
and raw—no reason for the huddled man
to be let in, to tell of loves he's had
before, and lack the means himself to stand—

A wind-soaked beggar, broken stringed across the path;
no gleam upon the hill to bring him home at last.

First published in *Envoi Magazine*, Autumn 2014

Hope

I have lived with long nights, long years alone,
embraced them all, my many loves, and took
to wife a silent, dull and senseless one
with fingers prising out a second look.

In trying not to know you, kept your name
even from myself, slipped it silently
into the river, into the dark flame,
turning my taloned shoulder like a key.

Ignoring even your absence, drawing
your signs like venom to be sucked and spat;
flooring with a shoulder slam, the roaring
bear within my blood; knocked desire flat.

Still you are there, a breath not taken in,
but wait for me to fill my lungs again

June, First Thing In The Morning

This girl of gold slips quiet through my window,
drips kisses on my eyes, and lying warm
upon my skin, entices from the shadows,
a whimpered heart, and somehow free of harm.

Another night has passed: long hours spent
within her absence, coldly in the dark:
a naked man of bone and nail, intent
on every knife-fight, cry and foxes' bark,

pulling wings from every minute, tying
crackers to the shirt-tails of the moon,
drowning hours in a bag, defying
sleep's administration and calming tune,

upon my shabby bed, neglected lain,
surprised as always, find her come again.

The Empty Aviary

Write me a poem, and let it be truth
enough to raise a heart, still beating, out
of an untended cage; for each beat to be
a rapture remembered, with a down-sweep

of feathers and the muscle of wings; a lightness
which says this beauty is freedom; strokes
as lifting as effortless bone, as breath,
abandoning weight to the cage's keep.

Then, let it release, take flight from your hands,
in a cock-sparrow dash and a billow of dove,
in the slow appraising climb of an eagle,
wild in the sky, and no longer seen...

with what remains—this ink on the page—
the scratchings of a captured bird, now free

About The Poet

Math Jones worked as a bookseller in Worcester for several years before retraining as an actor. He'd written sporadically throughout his earlier life, yet it was in Worcester, amidst a lively and passionate literary circle, that the commitment towards poetry really took root. Finding ready opportunities in the county and West Midlands to perform, and making good use of his theatrical flair, his work has become both dramatic and intimate, modern and traditional, mythological and intensely personal. Based again in his native London, he often returns to Worcester to share his newest writings.